by Chat Mingkwan

A collection of delectable Thai dishes, from delicious Crispy Shrimp Cakes to flavorful Shredded Chicken Salad and Stir-fried Beef with Basil, this book will delight all Thai food lovers.

PERIPLUS

Introduction

As the youngest in the family living in Bangkok, I was often left behind to help out in the kitchen while my older brothers and sisters ran off to play. At first I did not look forward to cooking, but later learned to enjoy it, as I acquired the skills and joy of cooking. I can still remember how thrill I was when I intentionally prepared my siblings' meals with excessive spiciness and still got away with it. The food was so delicious that they were unsure whether to punish or praise me.

My culinary skills were gained from helping my aunt with the cooking, in the same way she developed hers from her previous generation, as in any Thai household. Every Thai family has developed slightly different recipes due to individual tastes and preferences. In the old days, the housewife was always the matriarch of the family. She would get up early to prepare breakfast. After seeing her family members off to work or to schools, she would make a trip to a local market to pick up the freshest produce to cook for the day. Her dinner menu usually offered 4 to 5 dishes depending on the size of her family and often included a salad with lots of vegetables, a soup of clear broth or coconut base, a stir-fried of meat and mixed vegetables, and a sweet dish or fresh fruits for a dessert. In a traditional Thai family with three generations living under one roof, family members were often recruited to help in the kitchen. Helpers inadvertently became apprentices under her guidance and to continue her cooking traditions. Recipes were sometimes regarded as a family heirloom and a family secret.

Such homestyle cooking is still prevalent throughout Thailand today but is no longer in the grand scale as it used to be, as Thai families are getting smaller. Family members, including the housewives, are spending more time away from home and the cooking chore is naturally reduced both in the time spent and quantity of food. After returning home, family members usually pitch in to cook their dinner. Homestyle cooking has evolved to fit new lifestyles, technologies and ingredients. The family's cook doesn't have to shop every day, as refrigerators are now available to preserve cooking ingredients. Modern kitchen devices have speeded up food preparations, making the task of cooking less laborious. Food can now be cooked in small portions for single meals or in large quantities to last for several meals. New ingredients and cooking techniques introduced through trade with other countries have added new varieties to Thai home cooked meals.

Homestyle cooking is always considered very specialized, imbued a great deal with the cook's personality and family preferences. A meal cooked in small portions is carefully executed in details and the taste is adjusted to the family liking. Ingredients are specifically selected and the tastes are highly individualized in contrast to restaurant meals that appeal to the masses.

In this book, I have selected more than 30 Thai dishes that are perfect for homestyle cooking. These are featured in easy-to-follow recipes that are suited for all levels of skills, providing you with a useful guide to whip up a satisfying meal for your family.

Thai basil (*horapa*)

Lemon basil (*manglak*)

Holy basil (*kaprow*)

Basil is used as a seasoning and garnish in Thai cooking. Three varieties are often used. **Thai basil** (*horapa*) tastes rather like Italian sweet basil with a hint of anise and is used in red and green curries. It is available year round. **Lemon basil** (*manglak*) has a lemony flavor that goes well with soups and salads, especially with *Kanom Jeen* curry noodles. **Holy basil** or **hot basil** (*kaprow*) has distinctive purple-reddish leaves and a mint-like zesty flavor and is used for stir-fries such as *Pad Bai Kaprow*. Holy basil is hard to find and mostly available during the midsummer months. Basil doesn't store well, so buy it just before you intend to use it. European sweet basil can be used as a substitute for all varieties if you can't find the Thai varieties. Basil has a strong flavor, so don't use more than the recipe states.

Dried red chilies

Fresh red chilies

Bird's-eye chilies

Chilies are indispensable in Thai cooking and many different varieties are used. The large, finger-length green, red or yellow chili is moderately hot. **Dried red chilies** of this variety are ground to make chili flakes or ground red pepper. Tiny red, green or yellowy-orange **bird's-eye chilies** are extremely hot and are used in soups, curries and sauces. They are also available dried.

Chinese celery is much smaller with thinner stems than the normal Western variety and has a very intense, parsley-like flavor. The leaves and sometimes the stems are added to soups, rice dishes and stir-fried vegetables.

Coconut cream and **coconut milk** are used in many Thai desserts and curries. To obtain fresh coconut cream, grate the flesh of 1 coconut into a bowl (this will yield about 4 cups of grated coconut flesh), add $^{1}/_{2}$ cup water and knead thoroughly a few times, then strain with a muslin cloth or cheesecloth. **Thick coconut milk** is obtained by the same method but by adding double the water to the grated flesh (about 1 cup instead of $^{1}/_{2}$ cup). **Thin coconut milk** (which is used for soups and curries rather than desserts) is obtained by pressing the coconut a second time, adding 1 cup of water to the same grated coconut flesh and squeezing it again. You may also obtain thin coconut milk by diluting the thick coconut milk with water. Although freshly pressed milk has a better flavor, coconut cream and milk are now widely sold canned or in packets that are quick and convenient.

Coriander leaves with roots and stems

Coriander is the most common herb used in Thai cooking. The whole plant is used—the root, stem and leaves. **Coriander seeds** are roasted and then ground in a spice mill and used in curry pastes. **Coriander roots** are ground in spice pastes, while **coriander leaves** (also known as cilantro or Chinese parsley) are used for their fresh flavor, and as a garnish. For storage, wash and dry the fresh leaves before placing them in a plastic bag in the refrigerator—they will keep for 5 to 6 days.

Fish sauce is indispensable in Thai cooking. Made from salted, fermented fish or prawns, good quality fish sauce is golden-brown in color and has a salty tang. It is used in the same way as the Chinese use soy sauce.

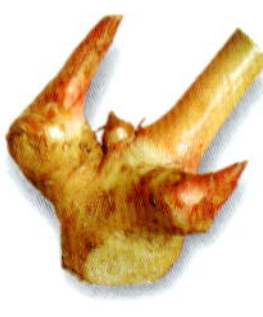

Galangal is a rhizome similar to ginger in appearance and a member of the same family. Known as *kha* in Thailand, *laos* in Indonesia and *lengkuas* in Singapore and Malaysia, it adds a distinctive fragrance and flavor to many Thai dishes. Dried galangal lacks the fragrance of fresh galangal, and most food stores now sell it fresh. It can be sliced and kept sealed in the freezer for several months.

Green peppercorns are fresh peppercorn berries that are available still on the vine or bottled or canned in a brine. The peppercorns should be drained and rinsed before using. Thai and European varieties are readily available.

Kaffir lime is a small lime that has a very knobby and intensely fragrant skin, but virtually no juice. The skin or rind is often grated and added to dishes as a seasoning. The fragrant **kaffir lime leaves** are added whole to soups and curries, or finely shredded and added to salads or deep-fried fish cakes, giving a wonderfully tangy taste to these dishes. They are available frozen or dried in Asian food stores; frozen leaves are much more flavorful than dried ones. The dried rind can be reconstituted and substituted for fresh.

Krachai or Chinese keys is a rhizome widely cultivated in Thailand. It gives a subtle spicy flavor to dishes and goes well with seafood. Fresh *krachai* is beige in color and looks like a bunch of baby carrots. Buy smooth and firm rhizomes. Store in a paper bag in the refrigerator for up to a few weeks. Preserved *krachai* is sold in jars either whole or cut into strips.

Lemongrass or citronella is a lemon-scented stem which grows in clumps. Each plant resembles a miniature leek. Use only the thicker bottom one third of the lemongrass stem, remove and discard the dry outer leaves and use only the tender inner part of the stem. Lemongrass is available fresh in most supermarkets.

Palm sugar is made from the distilled juice of various palm fruits. Palm sugar varies in color from golden to dark brown. It has a rich flavor similar to dark brown sugar or maple syrup, which makes a good substitute.

Rice vinegar is mild and faintly fragrant, and is the preferred vinegar throughout Southeast Asia. Chinese brands are inexpensive and widely available, while the Japanese rice vinegar, used in sushi, is sweeter and milder.

Rice wine is a relatively low alcohol content "rice beer" fermented from freshly steamed glutinous rice or millet. Widely used in Asian cooking, the Chinese rice wine is readily available in bottles in Asian markets. The Japanese rice wine, sake or the sweeter mirin and dry sherry can be used as substitutes.

Glass noodles
(*tang hoon*)

Kway teow
(rice sticks or *hofun*)

Fresh egg noodles
(*bami*)

Rice vermicelli
(*beehoon*)

Thai noodles are available in many forms, and are made from either rice, wheat or mung bean flour. **Kway teow**, also known as rice sticks or *hofun*, are wide, flat rice-flour noodles sold fresh in Asian markets and available in dried form elsewhere. If fresh *kway teow* cannot be obtained, use **dried rice stick noodles** instead (these must be blanched for 3 to 5 minutes and drained before using). **Dried rice vermicelli** are very fine rice threads that must also be soaked before using. **Egg noodles** (*bami*) are made from wheat flour and are similar to ramen, which may be used as a substitute. **Glass noodles**, also known as cellophane noodles, *tang hoon* or bean threads, are thin transparent noodles made from mung bean flour. They are sold in dried form and must be soaked in warm water to soften.

Shrimp paste or *belachan* is a dense mixture of fermented ground shrimp. It is sold in dried blocks and ranges from pink to blackish-brown in color. Shrimp paste should be slightly roasted to enhance its flavor before using. Traditionally, it is wrapped in banana leaves and roasted over embers for a few minutes. It may also be roasted directly over a low flame using tongs for 30 seconds or heated in a frying-pan, wrapped in aluminium foil, for 1 to 2 minutes. Alternatively it can also be microwaved very quickly in a bowl covered with plastic for 30 seconds or so. Do not overcook the shrimp paste or it will scorch, becoming bitter and dried.

Tapioca pearls are round pellets made from tapioca starch. They are sold in packets of large or fine pearls. Tapioca pearls have a soft and irresistibly chewy texture when cooked. They are used in making puddings and are added to drinks, as in the case of the well-known "bubble tea". Sago pearls (made from the inner pulp of a sago palm) are a good substitute.

Taucheo or salted soy bean paste is sold in jars and used as a salty seasoning. It is made from salted and fermented soy beans that are usually brownish in color. Some brands yield golden-brown beans and are labeled "yellow bean paste". "Sweet" and "hot" salted soy beans have added sugar and chili.

Tamarind is a sour fruit that comes in a hard pod. Tamarind juice is one of the major souring agents in Thai cooking. To make tamarind juice, mix 1 tablespoon of dried tamarind pulp with 2 tablespoons of warm water to soften, then mash well and strain to remove the seeds and fibers.

Water chestnut is a tuber that resembles a chestnut in color and shape. Available fresh, processed and canned, this firm and crispy textured Chinese vegetable is easily sourced in supermarkets and Asian stores. Store soaking in water in the refrigerator for up to a week.

Spicy Steamed Fish Parcels

6 large banana leaf sheets, soaked in hot water until soft or 1 baking pan (20 x 20 cm/8 x 8 in)
Toothpicks or staples, for fastening
500 ml (2 cups) water
$^{1}/_{4}$ teaspoon salt
300 g (10 oz) Chinese cabbage, shredded to yield 3 cups
500 g (1 lb) white fish fillets (catfish, snapper, grouper or mackerel)
2 tablespoons fish sauce
250 ml (1 cup) thick coconut milk
4 kaffir lime leaves, thinly sliced into fine strips
1 egg, beaten
2 tablespoons cornstarch
$^{1}/_{4}$ teaspoon salt
Sprigs of coriander leaves (cilantro), to garnish

Chili Paste
5 to 8 dried red chilies, soaked in warm water for 15 minutes until soft, stems discarded, deseeded
2 red chilies, deseeded and sliced
2 stalks lemongrass, thick bottom part only, outer layers discarded, inner part sliced
2 kaffir lime leaves
$2^{1}/_{2}$ cm (1 in) galangal root, peeled and sliced
5 cm (2 in) *krachai* (Chinese keys) or young ginger, peeled and sliced
4 cloves garlic
6 shallots
1 teaspoon black peppercorns
1 teaspoon dried shrimp paste
1 teaspoon salt

Makes 12 parcels
Preparation time: **1 hour**
Cooking time: **25 mins**

1 Make the Chili Paste first by grinding all the ingredients to a smooth paste in a blender or food processor, adding some water to keep the blades turning if necessary. Transfer to a bowl and set aside.
2 Cut out twenty-four 18-cm (7-in) circles from the banana leaf sheets. To make a banana leaf cup, lay 2 circles on top of one another and fold up the edges to form a cup, fastening the folded corners with toothpicks or staples. Continue with the remaining circles to make a total of 12 cups.
3 Bring the water and salt to a boil in a pot and blanch the cabbage for 2 to 3 minutes until tender. Drain and set aside.
4 Mince $^{1}/_{4}$ of the fish fillets and slice the remaining $^{3}/_{4}$ into thin pieces. Set aside.
5 Combine the minced fish, fish sauce and Chili Paste in a mixing bowl and mix until well blended. Add $^{1}/_{2}$ of the thick coconut milk, a little at a time, stirring to mix well. Add the fish pieces, kaffir lime leaves and egg, and mix until well combined.
6 Line each banana leaf cup with some cabbage and spoon the fish mixture over until $^{2}/_{3}$ full. If using a baking pan, lightly grease the pan and place all the cabbage in the pan and top with the fish mixture.
7 Combine the remaining coconut milk, cornstarch and salt in a bowl and mix well. Spread 2 tablespoons of the coconut mixture over the fish mixture in each banana leaf cup or all of the coconut mixture in the baking pan.
8 Place the fish parcels or baking pan in a steamer, cover and steam for 15 to 20 minutes until cooked. Serve hot, garnished with coriander leaves (cilantro).

Crispy Shrimp Cakes (Tod Mun Goong)

500 g (1 lb) fresh prawns or shrimp, peeled and deveined
150 g (5 oz) ground pork (optional)
$^1/_2$ teaspoon salt
1 tablespoon fish sauce
1 tablespoon sugar
$^1/_4$ teaspoon ground white pepper
60 g (1 cup) breadcrumbs
Oil for deep-frying
2 pieces fresh pineapple, thinly sliced, to garnish (optional)
Chinese plum sauce, to serve (optional)

Sweet Thai Chili Sauce
2 tablespoons water
2 tablespoons fish sauce
100 g ($^1/_2$ cup) sugar
$^1/_2$ cucumber, halved and thinly sliced
1 tablespoon minced garlic
1 teaspoon minced red chili
60 ml ($^1/_4$ cup) rice vinegar
4 tablespoons chopped roasted unsalted peanuts
$^1/_4$ teaspoon salt
Sprigs of coriander leaves (cilantro), to garnish

1 To make the Sweet Thai Chili Sauce, bring the water, fish sauce and sugar to a boil in a saucepan over medium heat, and simmer for 2 to 3 minutes, stirring constantly, until the mixture turns into a thin syrup. Remove from the heat and set aside. About 10 minutes before serving, combine all the other ingredients with the syrup and mix well. Transfer to a serving bowl.
2 Grind the peeled prawns or shrimp to a paste in a food processor. Combine the prawns or shrimp, pork (if using), salt, fish sauce, sugar and pepper in a large bowl and mix until well blended.
3 Wet your hands, spoon 1 tablespoon of the mixture and shape it into a ball, then press it flat to form a round cake. Coat the cake on all sides with the breadcrumbs. Continue until all the mixture is used up.
4 Heat the oil in a wok or saucepan until hot. Gradually lower the coated cakes into the oil, a few at a time, and deep-fry for about 5 minutes, turning occasionally, until golden brown on all sides. Remove and drain on paper towels.
5 Line a serving platter with the pineapple slices (if using) and arrange the deep-fried cakes on top. Serve hot with a bowl of Sweet Thai Chili Sauce or Chinese plum sauce (if using) on the side.

Serves 4 to 6
Preparation time: **30 mins**
Cooking time: **20 mins**

Grilled Pork Satays

500 g (1 lb) pork loin, sliced into thin strips
30 bamboo skewers, soaked in water for 1 hour before using
2 tablespoons oil, for basting when grilling
Sweet Thai Chili Sauce (page 8), for dipping (optional)
Sprigs of coriander leaves (cilantro), to garnish

Serves 4 to 6
Preparation time: **30 mins**
Cooking time: **20 mins**

Marinade
2 tablespoons minced garlic
2 tablespoons crushed coriander roots and stems
1 tablespoon ground coriander powder
1 teaspoon ground white pepper
2 tablespoons sugar
80 ml ($^1/_3$ cup) thick coconut milk
1 tablespoon fish sauce

Tangy Dipping Sauce
3 tablespoons fish sauce
3 tablespoons freshly squeezed lime or lemon juice
1 tablespoon sugar
1 tablespoon minced red chili
1 tablespoon thinly sliced garlic
1 tablespoon thinly sliced shallots
1 tablespoon minced coriander leaves (cilantro)
1 tablespoon sliced spring onion

1 Make the Marinade first by combining all the ingredients in a large bowl and mixing well. Add the pork strips to the Marinade, mix until well coated and marinate for at least 3 hours or overnight if possible.
2 To make the Tangy Dipping Sauce, combine all the ingredients in a serving bowl and stir until the sugar is dissolved. Dilute with some water if desired. Set aside.
3 Thread each marinated pork strip onto a bamboo skewer. Thread all the pork strips in this manner and grill, a few at a time, on a pan grill or under a preheated broiler wing for 3 to 5 minutes on each side, brushing with a little oil, until cooked. Transfer to a serving platter.
4 Serve hot as a snack with a bowl of Tangy Dipping Sauce or Sweet Thai Chili Sauce (page 8), garnished with coriander leaves, or serve as a main course with steamed rice.

To save time, you may place the pork skewers on a tray, brush with a little oil and grill in the oven for about 8 minutes on each side.

Crab Dumplings and Baby Bok Choy in Clear Soup

25 wonton wrappers
500 g (1 lb) baby bok choy, cleaned and halved lengthwise
Crispy Fried Shallots (page 29), to serve
1 spring onion, thinly sliced, to garnish
Sprigs of coriander leaves (cilantro), to garnish

Serves 4 to 6
Preparation time: **50 mins**
Cooking time: **30 mins**

Filling
250 g (9 oz) crabmeat
1 tablespoon soy sauce
1 tablespoon rice wine or sherry
1 tablespoon sugar
1 teaspoon sesame oil
2 teaspoons cornstarch
4 water chestnuts (about 125 g/4 oz), peeled and diced
2 tablespoons thinly sliced spring onions
1 tablespoon minced coriander leaves (cilantro)
$^{1}/_{4}$ chicken stock cube, dissolved in 1 tablespoon hot water

Broth
1$^{1}/_{2}$ liters (6 cups) chicken stock or 2 to 3 stock cubes dissolved in 1$^{1}/_{2}$ liters (6 cups) hot water
3 tablespoons crushed coriander roots and stems
4 stalks (40 g) Chinese celery, chopped to yield 1 cup
1 small onion, diced
1 teaspoon ground white pepper
3 tablespoons rice wine or sherry
2 tablespoons soy sauce
1 teaspoon salt
1 tablespoon freshly squeezed lime juice

1 To make the Filling, combine all the ingredients in a bowl and mix well. Cover with a cloth and allow to marinate for at least 30 minutes in the refrigerator.
2 To make the Broth, bring the chicken stock to a boil in a stockpot. Add the coriander roots and stems, Chinese celery and onion, and simmer for 10 to 15 minutes. Remove from the heat and strain the solids from the stock using a fine sieve. Discard the solids and return the clear Broth to the stove. Season the clear Broth with all the other ingredients and keep it hot over very low heat.
3 To make the dumplings, place 1 heaping teaspoon of the Filling onto the center of a wonton wrapper and dab the edges with a little water. Fold the wrapper in half to form a semicircle, enclosing the Filling, and press the edges together to seal. If using a square wrapper, fold in half diagonally to form a triangle. Repeat until all the ingredients are used up.
4 Bring a pot of water to a boil over high heat. Blanch the baby bok choy for about 2 minutes. Remove and drain.
5 Bring the same pot of water to a boil again and add the dumplings, a few at a time and making sure that they do not stick together. Boil the dumplings for 2 to 4 minutes until they float to the surface. Remove with a slotted spoon and drain.
6 Place the dumplings and bok choy in individual serving bowls, pour the hot Broth over and serve hot, sprinkled with Crispy Fried Shallots, spring onion and coriander leaves.

Crispy Fried Meatballs with Sweet Chili Sauce

200 g (7 oz) dried egg noodles (*bami*) or ramen
Oil for deep-frying
Sweet Thai Chili Sauce (page 8)

Filling
250 g (9 oz) fresh prawns, peeled and deveined
250 g (9 oz) ground pork or chicken
1 tablespoon minced garlic
1 tablespoon crushed coriander roots and stems
1 tablespoon minced shallots
1 egg, beaten
1 tablespoon soy sauce
1 tablespoon fish sauce
1 tablespoon sugar
$^1/_4$ teaspoon ground white pepper
$^1/_4$ chicken stock cube, dissolved in 1 tablespoon hot water
4 water chestnuts (about 120 g), peeled and diced to yield $^1/_2$ cup
4 tablespoons minced coriander leaves (cilantro)
2 tablespoons cornstarch

1 To make the Filling, grind the prawns to a paste in a food processor, then combine with all the other ingredients in a bowl and mix well. Set aside.
2 Bring a pot of water to a boil over medium heat. Blanch the noodles for 3 to 5 minutes until soft. Remove and plunge in cold water. Drain and set aside.
3 Wet your hands, spoon 1 heaping tablespoon of the Filling and shape it into a ball. Coil 7 to 10 noodles around the ball, making sure that it is completely wrapped. Continue until all the Filling is used up.
4 Heat the oil in a wok over medium heat until very hot and gently lower the noodle balls into the oil, a few at a time, making sure that the noodles stick to the Filling. Deep-fry for 5 to 7 minutes each, turning occasionally, until crispy and golden brown on all sides. Remove and drain on paper towels.
5 Arrange the crunchy noodle balls on a serving platter and serve with Sweet Thai Chili Sauce (page 8).

Makes 22 balls
Preparation time: **35 mins**
Cooking time: **20 mins**

Shredded Chicken Salad

375 ml ($1^1/_2$ cups) water
$^1/_4$ teaspoon salt
300 g (10 oz) boneless chicken breasts
300 g (10 oz) Chinese cabbage, thinly sliced to yield 3 cups
$^1/_2$ small carrot (about 50 g), peeled and grated
40 g (1 cup) fresh mint leaves, thinly sliced
3 tablespoons thinly sliced Thai basil leaves (*horapa*)
3 tablespoons coarsely chopped roasted unsalted peanuts, to serve
Sprigs of coriander leaves (cilantro), to garnish
2 tablespoons thinly sliced spring onions, to garnish
Crispy Fried Shallots (page 29), to garnish

Dressing
1 tablespoon minced red chili
1 tablespoon minced garlic
2 tablespoons sugar
3 tablespoons freshly squeezed lime juice
2 tablespoons fish sauce

1 Combine the Dressing ingredients in a bowl and mix well. Set aside.
2 Bring the water and salt to a boil in a saucepan or small pot over medium heat, and poach the chicken for about 15 minutes until cooked. Remove and set aside to cool. Shred the chicken along the grain into long thin strips.
3 Combine the chicken strips, cabbage, carrot, mint and basil in a mixing bowl and gently toss to mix well, adding the Dressing a little at a time.
4 Transfer the salad to a serving platter and sprinkle the peanuts on top. Serve immediately, garnished with coriander leaves, green onion and Crispy Fried Shallots (page 29).

Serves 4 to 6
Preparation time: **35 mins**
Cooking time: **15 mins**

Catfish Salad with Green Apple and Mango

125 ml ($^1/_2$ cup) water
$^1/_4$ teaspoon salt
500 g (1 lb) catfish fillets
Oil for deep-frying
1 unripe mango, peeled and cut into sticks
1 green apple, cut into sticks
1 small onion, halved and thinly sliced
125 g (4 oz) lettuce, torn to yield 2 cups
4 tablespoons coarsely chopped roasted unsalted peanuts, to garnish
Sprigs of coriander leaves (cilantro), to garnish

Dressing
60 ml ($^1/_4$ cup) fish sauce
60 ml ($^1/_4$ cup) freshly squeezed lime juice
3 tablespoons shaved palm sugar or brown sugar
1 tablespoon sliced red chili

1 Combine all the Dressing ingredients in a bowl and mix until the sugar is dissolved. Set aside.
2 Bring the water and salt to a boil in a wok or skillet, and poach the fish fillets over medium low heat for about 5 minutes until cooked. Remove from the heat and pat the fillets dry with paper towels. Place the fillets on a tray. Using a fork, shred the fillets into rough and fuzzy strands. Set aside to dry for 30 minutes.
3 Heat the oil in a wok until hot. Drop the fish strands into the hot oil at different spots and deep-fry for 3 to 5 minutes, turning once, until puffed, crispy and golden brown on all sides. Remove with a wire mesh or slotted spoon and drain on paper towels.
4 Combine the deep-fried puffed fish, mango, apple and onion in a mixing bowl and gently toss to mix well, adding the Dressing a little at a time.
5 To serve, line a serving platter with shredded lettuce, top with the fish mixture and garnish with peanuts and coriander leaves. Alternatively, serve individually in layers of ingredients with the deed-fried puffed fish on top and a bowl of Dressing on the side.

If catfish is not available, use 1 can of tuna chunks instead. Do not poach the tuna, just drain and shred, then deep-try in the same manner.

Serves 6 to 8
Preparation time: **30 mins**
Cooking time: **10 mins**

Glass Noodle Soup with Mushrooms and Meatballs

150 g (5 oz) dried glass noodles (*tang hoon*)
6 dried black Chinese mushrooms, soaked in warm water for 20 minutes until soft, stems discarded and caps sliced to yield 1 cup
Ground white pepper
Sprigs of coriander leaves (cilantro), to garnish
2 spring onions, thinly sliced, to garnish

Meatballs
250 g (9 oz) lean ground pork
2 tablespoons crushed coriander roots and stems
1 tablespoon minced garlic
1 tablespoon minced shallots
1 teaspoon ground white pepper
1 tablespoon fish sauce
1 tablespoon soy sauce

Broth
$1^1/_2$ liters (6 cups) chicken stock or 2 to 3 stock cubes dissolved in $1^1/_2$ liters (6 cups) hot water
3 tablespoons crushed coriander roots and stems
1 teaspoon ground white pepper
3 tablespoons rice wine or sherry
2 tablespoons soy sauce
1 tablespoon fish sauce
1 tablespoon chopped preserved daikon radish (*chai po*)

Serves 4
Preparation time: **30 mins**
Cooking time: **25 mins**

1 To make the Meatballs, combine all the ingredients in a bowl and mix until well blended. Wet your hands, spoon 1 tablespoon of the mixture and shape it into a ball. Continue until all the pork mixture is used up.
2 Make the Broth by bringing the chicken stock to a boil in a stockpot over high heat. Add all the other ingredients and bring the mixture to a boil once again. Add the Meatballs and simmer for 5 to 7 minutes, stirring occasionally, until they are cooked. Add the glass noodles and mushrooms and simmer for about 5 minutes, until the noodles are soft and transparent. Remove from the heat.
3 Transfer to individual serving bowls, sprinkle with pepper and serve hot, garnished with coriander leaves and spring onion.

Preserved daikon radish *(chai po), also known as Chinese pickled turnip or radish, is sugar- and salt-cured daikon radish. It is salty and sweet, and has a crunchy texture. Commonly used in Chinese dishes, preserved radish is available in the dried food section of all Asian markets.*

Egg Noodle Soup with Chicken and Bok Choy

375 ml ($1^1/_2$ cups) water
$^1/_4$ teaspoon salt
500 g (1 lb) boneless chicken breasts or Chinese BBQ pork (*char siew*)
500 g (1 lb) baby bok choy, quartered lengthwise
1 kg (2 lbs) fresh egg noodles or 500 g (1 lb) dried egg noodles
Crispy Fried Shallots (page 29), to serve
2 spring onions, sliced, to garnish
Sprigs of coriander leaves (cilantro), to garnish

Broth
$1^1/_2$ liters (6 cups) chicken stock or 2 to 3 chicken stock cubes dissolved in $1^1/_2$ liters (6 cups) hot water
3 tablespoons crushed coriander roots and stems
4 stalks (40 g) Chinese celery, chopped to yield about 1 cup
1 small red onion, diced
2 teaspoons ground white pepper
3 tablespoons rice wine or sherry
2 tablespoons soy sauce
1 teaspoon salt
1 tablespoon freshly squeezed lemon or lime juice (optional)

1 To make the Broth, bring the chicken stock to a boil in a stockpot over high heat. Add the coriander roots and stems, Chinese celery and onion, and simmer for 10 to 15 minutes. Remove from the heat and strain out the solids using a fine sieve. Discard the solids and return the clear Broth to the stove. Season with all the other ingredients and keep the Broth hot over very low heat.
2 Bring the water and salt to a boil in a saucepan and poach the chicken over medium heat for 10 to 15 minutes until cooked. Remove and set aside to cool. Slice the chicken into bite-sized pieces. If using the BBQ pork, slice thinly and set aside.
3 Bring a pot of water to a boil over high heat. Blanch the baby bok choy for about 2 minutes. Remove and drain. Set aside.
4 In the same pot of water, blanch the fresh egg noodles for 30 seconds, stirring constantly to separate the noodles. Remove and drain. If using dried egg noodles, blanch until soft, 3 to 5 minutes.
5 Place the egg noodles and baby bok choy in individual serving bowls. Pour the hot Broth over and top with the chicken pieces or BBQ pork, Crispy Fried Shallots, spring onion and coriander leaves. Serve hot.

Serves 4 to 6
Preparation time: **40 mins**
Cooking time: **30 mins**

Pork or Chicken with Green Beans in Red Curry

2 tablespoons oil
500 g (1 lb) fresh boneless chicken or pork, cut into bite-sized chunks
300 g (10 oz) green beans, cut into lengths to yield 3 cups
250 ml (1 cup) chicken stock or $^1/_4$ to $^1/_2$ chicken stock cube dissolved in 250 ml (1 cup) hot water
1 tablespoon fish sauce
2 tablespoons sugar
Kaffir lime leaves, thinly sliced into fine strips
$^1/_2$ red bell pepper, deseeded and thinly sliced
Sprigs of Thai basil (*horapa*)

Red Curry Paste
5 dried red chilies, soaked in warm water for 15 minutes until soft, stems discarded, deseeded
1 red chili, deseeded and sliced
5 shallots
2 cloves garlic
1 stalk lemongrass, thick bottom part only, outer layers discarded, inner part sliced
2 cm ($^3/_4$ in) galangal root, peeled and sliced
2 teaspoons crushed coriander roots and stems
$^1/_2$ teaspoon black peppercorns
1 kaffir lime leaf
$^1/_4$ teaspoon ground turmeric
$^1/_2$ teaspoon dried shrimp paste
$^1/_2$ teaspoon salt

Serves 4 to 6
Preparation time: **45 mins**
Cooking time: **20 mins**

1 To make the Red Curry Paste, grind all the ingredients to a smooth paste in a blender, adding some water to keep the blades turning if necessary.
2 Heat the oil in a wok or skillet over medium heat and stir-fry the Red Curry Paste for 3 to 5 minutes until fragrant. Increase the heat to high, add the chicken or pork and stir-fry for 3 to 5 minutes until almost cooked. Add the green beans and stir-fry for another 3 to 5 minutes until they are tender and cooked. Season with the chicken stock, fish sauce and sugar, and stir-fry for another 2 to 3 minutes before removing from the heat.
3 Transfer to a serving platter and sprinkle with kaffir lime leaves, red bell pepper and basil leaves. Serve hot with steamed rice.

Chicken Mussamun Curry (Mussamun Gai)

1 liter (4 cups) thin coconut milk and 125 ml ($^1/_2$ cup) thick coconut milk
1 fresh chicken (about 1 kg/2 lbs), cut into 12 pieces
3 cardamom pods
3 bay leaves
2 cinnamon sticks (each 8 cm/3 in)
3 medium potatoes, peeled and cubed
300 g (10 oz) pearl onions or 3 medium onions, chopped
50 g ($^1/_2$ cup) unsalted raw peanuts
3 tablespoons fish sauce
2 tablespoons shaved palm sugar or dark brown sugar
6 tablespoons tamarind juice (page 5)

Mussamun Curry Paste
3 dried red chilies, soaked in warm water for 15 minutes until soft, stems discarded, deseeded
$^3/_4$ tablespoon coriander seeds
$^3/_4$ teaspoon cumin seeds
2 cardamom pods
$^1/_2$ teaspoon ground nutmeg
2 cloves
1 cinnamon stick (3 cm/1 in) or $^1/_2$ teaspoon ground cinnamon
$^1/_2$ teaspoon black peppercorns
3 shallots
2 cloves garlic
1 stalk lemongrass, thick bottom part only, outer layers discarded, inner part sliced
1 cm ($^1/_2$ in) galangal root, peeled and sliced
$^1/_2$ tablespoon crushed coriander roots and stems
2 kaffir lime leaves
$^3/_4$ teaspoon dried shrimp paste
$^1/_2$ teaspoon salt
3 tablespoons water

Serves 6
Preparation time: **1 hour**
Cooking time: **45 mins**

1 To make the Mussamun Curry Paste, dry-fry the dried red chilies, coriander seeds, cumin, cardamom, nutmeg, cloves, cinnamon and black peppercorns in a wok or skillet over medium heat for about 5 minutes until fragrant. Combine the roasted ingredients and all the other ingredients and grind to a smooth paste in a blender.
2 Heat 60 ml ($^1/_4$ cup) of the thin coconut milk in a wok over medium heat until hot. Stir in the Mussamun Curry Paste and simmer for 2 to 3 minutes, stirring constantly, until fragrant.
3 Add the chicken and simmer for 2 to 3 minutes, basting with the curry. Add the remaining thin coconut milk, cardamom, bay leaves and cinnamon, mix well and bring to a boil. Reduce the heat to low and simmer for 25 to 30 minutes until the chicken is tender and cooked.
4 Increase the heat to medium, add the potatoes, onions, peanuts, fish sauce, palm sugar and tamarind juice, and simmer for about 20 minutes, stirring occasionally until the vegetables are cooked. Stir in the thick coconut milk and adjust for seasoning, adding more fish sauce, sugar and tamarind juice if desired. Simmer for another 5 to 7 minutes and remove from the heat.
5 Transfer to a serving bowl and serve hot with steamed rice.

Lemongrass Barbecue Chicken

1 fresh chicken (about 1 kg/2 lbs) or 4 to 6 chicken legs
Lemon wedges, to serve

Marinade
$^1/_2$ teaspoon salt
6 cloves garlic
1 teaspoon ground white pepper
3 tablespoons crushed coriander roots and stems
3 stalks lemongrass, thick bottom part only, outer layers discarded, inner part sliced

Fish Sauce Dip
25 g (1 cup) dried white-bait (*ikan bilis*) or 2 pieces (about 45 g) dried salted fish fillets
2 stalks lemongrass, thick bottom part only, outer layers discarded, inner part sliced
6 shallots
4 cloves garlic
$2^1/_2$ cm (1 in) galangal root, peeled and sliced
5 red chilies, deseeded and sliced
2 tablespoons tamarind juice (page 5)
60 ml ($^1/_4$ cup) fish sauce
1 tablespoon freshly squeezed lime juice
1 tablespoon sugar

1 Rinse and clean the chicken. If using a whole chicken, halve lengthwise and cut into 8 pieces.
2 Make the Marinade by grinding all the ingredients to a smooth paste in a blender. Rub the Marinade into the chicken pieces and allow to marinate in the refrigerator for at least 3 hours or overnight if possible.
3 To make the Fish Sauce Dip, remove the heads and flick out the dark intestinal tracts of the whitebait if necessary, then rinse and drain. If using dried salted fish, boil the fish pieces in 250 ml (1 cup) of water over medium heat until the water reduces to half, about 10 minutes. Remove and drain. Dry-fry the whitebait or salted fish, lemongrass, shallots, garlic, galangal and chilies in a wok or skillet over medium heat for 5 to 7 minutes, until fragrant. Remove and grind in a blender until fine. Add all the other ingredients and mix until well combined. Dilute with some water if desired. Transfer to a serving bowl and set aside.
4 Grill the marinated chicken pieces on a pan grill or under a preheated broiler wing over medium heat for 7 to 10 minutes on each side, until golden brown and cooked. Transfer to a serving platter.
5 Serve hot with lemon wedges and a bowl of the Fish Sauce Dip on the side.

Dried whitebait (ikan bilis) *or silver fish is available in Asian stores either whole or cleaned, range from $1^1/_2$ cm to 6 cm (1 in to $2^1/_2$ in) in length. They are salted and sun-dried to make a seasoning and snack item. Buy packets that do not look powdery or stale. Store in a tightly closed container on the shelf.*

Serves 4
Preparation time: **50 mins**
Cooking time: **30 mins**

Stir-fried Chicken with Cashew Nuts

3 tablespoons minced garlic
500 g (1 lb) boneless chicken breasts, cut into bite-sized pieces
1 medium onion, halved and thinly sliced to yield 1 cup
1 small carrot, peeled and cut into sticks to yield 1 cup
120 g (4 oz) green beans, cut into lengths to yield 1 cup
1 small bell pepper, deseeded and cut into strips to yield 1 cup
1 tablespoon fish sauce
2 tablespoons oyster sauce
1 tablespoon sugar
95 g ($^{3}/_{4}$ cup) roasted unsalted cashew nuts
1 spring onion, sliced, to garnish

Crispy Fried Dried Chilies
3 tablespoons oil
6 dried red chilies, soaked in warm water for 15 minutes until soft, stems discarded, deseeded and drained

1 Make the Crispy Fried Dried Chilies first by heating the oil in a wok over medium heat until hot and stir-fry the dried chilies for 1 to 2 minutes until fragrant and crispy. Remove the chilies and drain on paper towels. Set aside.
2 In the same wok, heat the leftover oil over medium heat and stir-fry the garlic for 1 to 2 minutes, until fragrant and golden brown. Add the chicken and stir-fry for about 3 minutes until cooked. Add the onion, carrot, green beans and bell pepper, and stir-fry for 3 to 5 minutes until the vegetables are tender. Season with the fish sauce, oyster sauce and sugar. Stir-fry for 3 more minutes and remove from the heat. Finally stir in the Crispy Fried Dried Chilies and cashew nuts.
3 Serve hot on a serving platter, garnished with spring onion.

Serves 4 to 6
Preparation time: **25 mins**
Cooking time: **15 mins**

Stir-fried Chicken with Pumpkin

1 teaspoon oil
2 tablespoons minced garlic
300 g (10 oz) boneless chicken breasts, thinly sliced
1 small pumpkin or butternut squash (about 500 g/1 lb), top cut off, deseeded, flesh scooped out and cubed to yield about 2 cups
2 tablespoons fish sauce
2 tablespoons sugar
60 ml ($^1/_4$ cup) water
2 eggs, beaten
1 teaspoon ground white pepper
1 spring onion, cut into lengths, to garnish (optional)

1 Heat the oil in a wok or skillet over medium heat and stir-fry the garlic for 1 to 2 minutes until fragrant and golden brown. Add the chicken and stir-fry for 3 to 4 minutes until cooked. Stir in the pumpkin cubes and season with the fish sauce, sugar and water. Cover the wok or skillet and simmer for 6 to 8 minutes until the pumpkin is tender. Do not overcook or the pumpkin will disintegrate. Add the eggs and stir-fry until well combined. Remove from the heat and transfer to a serving platter.
2 Top with a sprinkling of pepper and garnish with green onion (if using). Serve hot with steamed rice.

Serves 6
Preparation time: **30 mins**
Cooking time: **10 mins**

Stir-fried Beef with Basil

- 4 tablespoons oil
- 5 bunches holy basil (*kaprow*), stems removed to yield 2 cups
- 3 tablespoons minced garlic
- 4 tablespoons minced shallots
- 2 to 3 tablespoons minced red chilies
- 500 g (1 lb) beef sirloin or flank steak, thinly sliced
- 200 g (7 oz) green beans, cut into lengths to yield 2 cups
- 5 cm (2 in) young ginger, peeled and cut into thin strips
- 1 tablespoon fish sauce
- $1^1/_2$ tablespoons oyster sauce
- 1 tablespoon sugar
- 95 g ($^3/_4$ cup) roasted unsalted cashew nuts (optional)

1 Heat the oil in a wok or skillet over medium heat until hot and stir-fry $^1/_2$ of the basil leaves for 2 to 3 minutes until crispy. Remove and drain on paper towels. Set aside.

2 In the same wok, heat the leftover oil over medium heat and stir-fry the garlic, shallots and chilies for 2 to 3 minutes until fragrant. Add the beef and stir-fry for 2 to 3 minutes until just cooked. Add the green beans and ginger, and season with the fish sauce, oyster sauce and sugar. Continue to stir-fry for another 2 to 3 minutes until the green beans are tender and cooked. Stir in the remaining basil leaves and remove from the heat.

3 Transfer to a serving platter, garnish with cashew nuts (if using) and the reserved crispy fried basil leaves, and serve hot with steamed rice.

Serves 4
Preparation time: **30 mins**
Cooking time: **15 mins**

Fragrant Beef Panaeng Curry

500 ml (2 cups) thin coconut milk and 125 ml ($^1/_2$ cup) thick coconut milk
700 g ($1^1/_2$ lbs) beef, cubed
4 tablespoons fish sauce
2 tablespoons shaved palm sugar or dark brown sugar
1 medium onion, halved and sliced
1 bell pepper, deseeded and cut into sticks
3 tablespoons ground roasted unsalted peanuts
4 kaffir lime leaves, thinly sliced into strips
Sprigs of Thai basil (*horapa*)

Panaeng Curry Paste
4 dried red chilies, soaked in warm water for 15 minutes until soft, stems discarded, deseeded
1 teaspoon coriander seeds
1 teaspoon cumin seeds
$^1/_2$ teaspoon black peppercorns
3 shallots
2 cloves garlic
1 stalk lemongrass, thick bottom part only, outer layers discarded, inner part sliced
1 cm ($^1/_2$ in) galangal root, peeled and sliced
1 teaspoon crushed coriander roots and stems
2 kaffir lime leaves
$^1/_2$ teaspoon dried shrimp paste
$^1/_4$ teaspoon salt
1 tablespoon chopped roasted unsalted peanuts
2 tablespoons water

Serves 6 to 8
Preparation time: **40 mins**
Cooking time: **50 mins**

1 To make the Panaeng Curry Paste, dry-fry the dried red chilies, coriander, cumin and black peppercorns in a wok or skillet over medium heat for about 5 minutes, until fragrant. Combine the roasted ingredients and all the other ingredients and grind to a smooth paste in a blender.
2 Heat 60 ml ($^1/_4$ cup) of the thin coconut milk in a wok over medium heat until hot. Stir in the Panaeng Curry Paste and simmer for 2 to 3 minutes, stirring constantly, until fragrant.
3 Add the beef cubes and simmer for 2 to 3 minutes, basting with the curry. Add the remaining thin coconut milk, fish sauce and palm sugar, mix well and bring to a boil. Reduce the heat to low and simmer for 40 minutes until the curry has reduced to half and the beef is tender.
4 Increase the heat to medium, add the onion, bell pepper and thick coconut milk and simmer for 7 to 10 minutes, stirring occasionally until the vegetables are cooked. Stir in the peanuts and remove from the heat.
5 Transfer to a serving bowl and sprinkle with kaffir lime leaves and basil leaves before serving.

Clear Lemongrass Soup with Beef and Cabbage

300 g (10 oz) beef fillets, top or bottom round, cubed
1 1/2 liters (6 cups) water
6 thin slices galangal root
3 stalks lemongrass, thick bottom part only, outer layers discarded, inner parts cut into lengths, bruised
5 kaffir lime leaves
2 tablespoons uncooked rice grains
4 tablespoons fish sauce
1 beef stock cube
1 tablespoon sugar (optional)
2 tablespoons thinly sliced shallots
4 tablespoons freshly squeezed lime juice
3 bunches Thai basil (*horapa*), stems removed
200 g (7 oz) Chinese cabbage, sliced to yield 2 cups
Sprigs of coriander leaves (cilantro), to garnish
2 tablespoons sliced spring onion, to garnish
Dried chili flakes, to serve

1 Bring the beef, water, galangal, lemongrass and kaffir lime leaves to a boil in a stockpot over high heat. Reduce heat to low, cover the stockpot and simmer for about 1 hour, skimming off any foam that floats to the surface, until the beef is tender. Set aside.
2 Dry-fry the rice grains in a wok or skillet over medium heat for 7 to 10 minutes, until light brown and fragrant. Remove from the heat and set aside to cool, then coarsely grind the roasted rice in a food processor.
3 Bring the beef mixture to a boil over medium heat and season with the fish sauce and stock cube. Remove from the heat, add the ground rice, sugar (if using), shallots and lime juice, and stir to mix well. Check seasoning, adding more fish sauce and lime juice if desired.
4 To serve, line the serving bowls with Thai basil and cabbage, pour the hot beef soup over and garnish with coriander leaves and spring onion. Serve hot with dried chili flakes.

Serves 6
Preparation time: **30 mins**
Cooking time: **1 hour 15 mins**

Fish in Fragrant Green Peppercorn Curry

500 ml (2 cups) thick coconut milk
500 g (1 lb) fish fillets
1 tablespoon fish sauce
1 tablespoon shaved palm sugar or dark brown sugar
4 tablespoons green peppercorns
5 kaffir lime leaves
2 tablespoons thinly sliced *krachai* or young ginger root, to garnish

Curry Paste
4 to 5 dried red chilies, soaked in warm water for 15 minutes until soft, stems discarded, deseeded
1 teaspoon coriander seeds
1 teaspoon cumin seeds
1 red chili, deseeded and sliced
2 shallots
2 cloves garlic
1 stalk lemongrass, thick bottom part only, outer layers discarded, inner part sliced
1 cm ($^1/_2$ in) galangal root, peeled and sliced
2 kaffir lime leaves, sliced
1 tablespoon crushed coriander roots and stems
1 teaspoon dried shrimp paste
$^1/_2$ teaspoon salt
60 ml ($^1/_4$ cup) water

1 To make the Curry Paste, dry-fry the dried red chilies, coriander seeds and cumin in a wok or skillet over medium heat for about 5 minutes until fragrant, taking care not to burn. Remove from the heat and set aside to cool. Combine the roasted ingredients and all the other ingredients and grind to a smooth paste in a blender.
2 Heat 125 ml ($^1/_2$ cup) of the coconut milk in a wok over medium heat until warmed through. Add the Curry Paste and simmer for 2 to 3 minutes, stirring from time to time, until fragrant. Add the fish and simmer for 2 to 3 minutes, basting with the curry. Add the remaining coconut milk along with the fish sauce, palm sugar, peppercorns and 3 kaffir lime leaves. Simmer for another 7 to 10 minutes until the fish is cooked and remove from the heat.
3 Very thinly slice the remaining kaffir lime leaves. Place the fish and curry on a serving platter, sprinkle the kaffir lime leaves and *krachai* or ginger on top, and serve hot with steamed rice.

Serves 4
Preparation time: **40 mins**
Cooking time: **30 mins**

Thai Sweet and Sour Prawns

3 tablespoons oil
3 tablespoons minced garlic
500 g (1 lb) fresh prawns, peeled and deveined
8 water chestnuts (about 200 g/7oz), peeled and diced to yield 1 cup
1 medium onion, diced to yield 1 cup
2 pieces fresh pineapple, diced to yield 1 cup
1 bell pepper, deseeded, diced to yield 1 $^{1}/_{2}$ cups
60 g ($^{1}/_{2}$ cup) roasted cashew nuts (optional)
Sprigs of coriander leaves (cilantro), to garnish

Sweet and Sour Sauce
2 tablespoons fish sauce
2 tablespoons oyster sauce
3 tablespoons sugar
3 tablespoons vinegar
2 tablespoons tomato sauce or ketchup
1 to 2 tablespoons chili sauce, *sambal oelek* or Sriracha sauce (optional)
1 tablespoon cornstarch
125 ml ($^{1}/_{2}$ cup) seafood stock or $^{1}/_{4}$ seafood stock cube dissolved in 125 ml ($^{1}/_{2}$ cup) hot water

1 To make the Sweet and Sour Sauce, mix all the ingredients in a bowl until well combined. Set aside.
2 Heat the oil in a wok over medium heat. Stir-fry the garlic for 1 to 2 minutes until golden brown and fragrant. Increase the heat to high, add the prawns and all the vegetables, and stir-fry for 2 to 3 minutes until just cooked. Add the Sweet and Sour Sauce and stir-fry for another 2 to 3 minutes until the sauce thickens and the ingredients are well coated. Finally stir-in the roasted cashew nuts and remove from the heat.
3 Transfer to a serving platter, garnish with coriander leaves and serve hot with steamed rice.

Serves 4 to 6
Preparation time: **50 mins**
Cooking time: **8 mins**

Fried Fish with Basil Leaves and Sweet Chili Sauce

1 whole fresh fish (about 1 kg/2 lbs)
1 teaspoon salt
Oil for deep-frying
Crispy Fried Basil Leaves (see note), to garnish
Crispy Fried Garlic (page 29), to garnish
Crispy Fried Shallots (page 29), to garnish
Crispy Fried Dried Chilies (page 38), to garnish

Sweet Chili Sauce
3 tablespoons minced garlic
3 tablespoons minced shallots
3 tablespoons crushed coriander roots and stems
2 tablespoons minced red chilies
2 tablespoons fish sauce
4 tablespoons shaved palm sugar
4 tablespoons tamarind juice (page 5)

1 Clean the fish and make 3 to 4 diagonal slits on each side. Rub the salt into the fish and set aside for 15 minutes, then rinse and drain. Pat dry with paper towels.
2 Heat the oil in a wok over high heat until very hot. Deep-fry the fish for 7 to 10 minutes, until golden brown and crispy on all sides. Remove and drain on paper towels. Transfer to a serving platter.
3 To make the Sweet Chili Sauce, heat 2 tablespoons of the oil in a wok or skillet over medium heat, stir-fry the garlic, shallots, coriander roots and stems, and chilies until fragrant, 3 to 5 minutes. Season with all the other ingredients and stir-fry for about 5 minutes, until the sugar is dissolved and the sauce is thick. Remove and pour the Sweet Chili Sauce over the fish.
4 Sprinkle the fish with Crispy Fried Basil, Crispy Fried Garlic (page 29), Crispy Fried Shallots (page 29) and Crispy Fried Dried Chilies (page 38), and serve hot.

*To make the **Crispy Fried Basil Leaves**, remove the stems from 15 sprigs of Thai basil (horapa) and stir-fry in 3 tablespoons of hot oil over medium heat for 1 to 2 minutes, stirring constantly, until fragrant and crispy. Remove with a slotted spoon and drain on paper towels.*

Serves 4
Preparation time: **45 mins**
Cooking time: **15 mins**

Mixed Seafood in Green Curry

750 ml (3 cups) thick coconut milk
200 g (7 oz) slender Asian eggplants, cubed to yield 2 cups
250 g (9 oz) zucchini, cubed to yield 2 cups
6 kaffir lime leaves
4 tablespoons fish sauce
1 tablespoon shaved palm sugar or dark brown sugar
250 g (9 oz) shucked fresh scallops, sliced
250 g (9 oz) fresh squids, cleaned, body sacs cut into rings
250 g (9 oz) fresh fish fillets, sliced
250 g (9 oz) mussels, scrubbed
Sprigs of Thai basil leaves (*horapa*), to garnish

Green Curry Paste
1 tablespoon cumin seeds
1 teaspoon coriander seeds
1/2 teaspoon black peppercorns
4 green chilies, deseeded and sliced
2 green bird's-eye chilies
1 stalk lemongrass, thick bottom part only, outer layers discarded, inner part sliced
1 cm (1/2 in) galangal root, peeled and sliced
1 kaffir lime leaf
4 shallots
2 cloves garlic
1 tablespoon crushed coriander roots and stems
1/2 teaspoon dried shrimp paste
1/2 teaspoon salt

Serves 4 to 6
Preparation time: **45 mins**
Cooking time: **20 mins**

1 To make the Green Curry Paste, dry-fry the cumin, coriander seeds and black peppercorns in a wok or skillet over medium heat for about 5 minutes, until fragrant. Combine the roasted ingredients and all the other ingredients and grind to a smooth paste in a blender.
2 Heat 60 ml (1/4 cup) of the coconut milk in a wok over medium heat until hot. Stir in the Green Curry Paste and simmer for 2 to 3 minutes, stirring constantly, until fragrant. Add the eggplant, zucchini and kaffir lime leaves and mix well. Add the remaining coconut milk and bring the curry to a boil. Season with the fish sauce and sugar. Reduce the heat to low and simmer for 7 to 10 minutes until the vegetables are cooked. Remove from the heat.
3 Just before serving, bring the curry to a boil over medium heat and add the seafood. Simmer for 2 to 3 minutes until the seafood is cooked. Check seasoning, adding more fish sauce and sugar if desired.
4 Transfer to a serving bowl and garnish with kaffir lime leaves. Serve hot with steamed rice.

Hot and Sour Seafood Soup

$1^1/_2$ liters (6 cups) seafood or chicken stock or 2 to 3 stock cubes dissolved in $1^1/_2$ liters (6 cups) hot water
3 stalks lemongrass, thick bottom part only, outer layers discarded, inner part cut into lengths and bruised
5 thin slices of galangal root
4 kaffir lime leaves
2 tablespoons fish sauce
1 tablespoon sugar
2 tablespoons Chili Paste (page 29)
125 g (4 oz) fresh prawns, peeled and deveined
125 g (4 oz) mussels, scrubbed and cleaned
125 g (4 oz) fish fillets, sliced
125 g (4 oz) squids, cleaned, body sacs cut into rings
100 g (3 oz) mushrooms, stems discarded, caps sliced
4 tablespoons freshly squeezed lime juice
1 tablespoon minced red chilies
2 tablespoons minced coriander leaves (cilantro), to garnish
2 tablespoons sliced spring onions, to garnish (optional)

1 Bring the stock to a boil in a stockpot over high heat. Add the lemongrass, galangal and kaffir lime leaves, and simmer for 10 to 15 minutes until the stock is infused with the herbs. Season with the fish sauce, sugar and Chili Paste and remove from the heat.
2 About 5 minutes before serving, bring the stock to a boil over high heat, add the seafood and mushrooms, and simmer for 3 to 5 minutes until cooked. Remove from the heat and stir in the lime juice and chilies. Check seasoning, adding more fish sauce, lime juice and Chili Paste if desired.
3 Serve hot in individual serving bowls, garnished with coriander leaves and spring onion (if using).

Serves 4
Preparation time: **30 mins**
Cooking time: **15 mins**

Peppercorn Prawn and Vegetable Soup

$1^1/_2$ liters (6 cups) seafood stock or 2 to 3 seafood stock cubes dissolved in $1^1/_2$ liters (6 cups) hot water
200 g (7 oz) pumpkin, deseeded, flesh cubed
200 g (7 oz) bottle gourd (see note) or zucchini, peeled and cubed
100 g (3 oz) baby corns, diced to yield 2 cups
100 g (3 oz) fresh mushrooms, stems discarded, caps diced
500 g (1 lb) fresh prawns, peeled and deveined
3 tablespoons fish sauce
1 tablespoon sugar
Sprigs of lemon basil (*manglak*), to garnish

Chili Paste
2 teaspoons black peppercorns
20 shallots
1 teaspoon dried shrimp paste
150 g (5 oz) fresh prawns, peeled and deveined, chopped to yield $^1/_2$ cup

1 To make the Chili Paste, grind the peppercorns, shallots and shrimp paste to a smooth paste in a blender. Add the prawns and pulse several times to mix well. Transfer to a bowl and set aside.
2 About 10 minutes before serving, bring the seafood stock to a boil in a stockpot over high heat and stir in the Chili Paste. Add the vegetables and simmer for 7 to 10 minutes, stirring occasionally, until cooked. Add the prawns and season with the fish sauce and sugar. Simmer for about 3 minutes, adjusting the seasoning by adding more fish sauce if desired, and remove from the heat.
3 Transfer to a serving bowl and garnish with basil leaves. Serve immediately with steamed rice.

Bottle Gourd *or Asian Gourd is a green long and slender vegetable similar to a green zucchini. Its ripped and tough skins need to be peeled before using. Mature bottle gourd has a dried hard shell and is water resistant.*

Serves 6
Preparation time: **60 mins**
Cooking time: **15 mins**

Fresh Mango Custard Tarts

12 tartlet molds (each 5 cm/2 in in diameter) or small cupcake molds
Whipped cream, for topping (optional)
50 g ($^1/_2$ cup) grated coconut, dry-roasted, to garnish (optional)

Pastry
150 g (1 cup) flour
50 g ($^1/_4$ cup) sugar
125 ml ($^1/_2$ cup) melted butter or shortening
$^1/_2$ egg, beaten
2 tablespoons thick coconut milk
1 teaspoon pandanus, vanilla, jasmine or rose essence

Filling
2 large or 3 medium ripe mangoes (about 500 g/1 lb in total), peeled, sliced
100 g ($^1/_2$ cup) sugar
250 ml (1 cup) thick coconut milk
60 g ($^1/_2$ cup) roasted unsalted cashew nuts, halved (optional)
2$^1/_2$ eggs, beaten
$^1/_2$ teaspoon freshly grated ginger
$^1/_2$ teaspoon ground cinnamon

1 Make the Pastry by combining all the ingredients in a mixing bowl and mixing well. Flour your hands and knead the mixture to a smooth dough on a floured surface. Using a rolling pin, roll the dough to a thin sheet, 3 mm ($^1/_8$ in) thick. From the dough sheet, cut out circles large enough to line the tartlet or cupcake molds. Flour each mold and line with a dough circle.
2 Preheat the oven to 210°C (420°F).
3 To make the Filling, process the mango slices to a puree in a blender. Whisk the sugar and coconut milk in a mixing bowl until the sugar is dissolved. Stir in the mango puree and cashew nuts, then add the eggs, ginger and cinnamon, and beat to mix well.
4 Spoon the Filling into each tartlet pan to almost full. Bake in the oven at 210°C(440°F) for about 10 minutes, then reduce the heat to 150°C(300°F) and bake for another 20 to 25 minutes, until the custard is set. Remove and set aside to cool.
5 Chill in the refrigerator for about 30 minutes. Top each tart with some whipped cream and garnish with grated coconut (if desired). Serve warm or at room temperature.

To save time, you may use the readymade pie crust or filo pastry instead of making your own.

Serves 6
Preparation time: 30 mins + 30 mins chilling
Cooking time: 25 mins

Bananas and Pumpkin in Rich Coconut Cream

- 1 liter (4 cups) thin coconut milk or 125 ml ($^1/_2$ cup) thick coconut milk
- 200 g (7 oz) pumpkin or yam or sweet potatoes, peeled, flesh cubed
- 5 large bananas or 12 baby bananas, peeled and halved lengthwise
- 90 g ($^1/_2$ cup) shaved palm sugar or dark brown sugar
- 1 teaspoon salt
- 1 teaspoon pandanus or vanilla essence

1 In a saucepan, bring the thin coconut milk slowly to a boil over medium heat. Add the pumpkin, yam or sweet potatoes and simmer uncovered for about 5 minutes until soft, then add the bananas and simmer for 3 more minutes. Stir in the palm sugar, salt and pandanus or vanilla essence, and mix until the sugar is completely dissolved. Simmer for 5 minutes and remove from the heat.

2 Add the thick coconut milk and mix until well combined. Serve hot or cold in individual serving bowls.

Serves 4
Preparation time: **10 mins**
Cooking time: **15 mins**

Tapioca Pearls with Tropical Fruits

1 liter (4 cups) water
150 g (1 cup) dried tapioca or sago pearls
250 ml (1 cup) fruit syrup, from canned fruits
200 g (1 cup) sugar
500 ml (2 cups) thick coconut milk
1 teaspoon pandanus or vanilla extract
Assorted tropical fruits (mango, lychee, jackfruit and mandarin orange), sliced to yield 4 cups
$^1/_4$ teaspoon salt
1 tablespoon cornstarch

1 Bring the water to a boil in a pot and add the tapioca or sago pearls. Simmer for 15 minutes over low heat, stirring constantly, until the pearls are soft and transparent. Add the fruit syrup, stir in $^1/_2$ of the sugar, $^1/_2$ of the coconut milk and the fragrant extract, and mix until the sugar is dissolved. Remove from the heat and add the sliced fruits, reserving some for garnishing.
2 To make the topping, combine the remaining sugar and coconut milk, salt and cornstarch in a saucepan and heat over medium heat, stirring constantly, until the mixture is thick, about 3 minutes. Remove and set aside.
3 Transfer the pudding to individual serving bowls and spread the topping on top. Garnish with the reserved sliced fruits and serve warm or cold.

Serves 10
Preparation time: **10 mins** Cooking time: **20 mins**

Complete List of Recipes